The Readers House

ISSUE 40
December 2023
thereadershouse.co.uk
Global edition

Master Minds Unveiled
Conversations with
Today's Literary Masters:

SARINA SIEBENALER
Inspiring Imaginations Through Words and Art
WAYNE MICHAEL HALL
Adaptation in Intelligence
RINA BROWN
An Indie Writer's Tale
RODNEY BOND
Journeys Through Universe
BARBARA GODIN
Unveiling Grace
GRACE ALLISON BLAIR
A Journey into Einstein's Compass and Beyond

Multi-Award Winning
UK Crime Novelist
SARAH HILARY
Unraveling Complex
Crime Narratives with
Remarkable Depth
INTERVIEW ☆

A Journey of Love, Family, and Fiction
SUSAN WIGGS
#1 New York Times Best Seller Author

Crafting Worlds, Inspiring Minds
JANICE HARDY
Author, Speaker, Educator

INTER
GO
Azure
SUS
Au
of

Dive

Into a Great Journey

Ready to
share
your
story?

The Reader's House
Make a phenomenal start
thereadershouse.co.uk

A good book will keep you fascinated for days. A good bookshop for your whole life.

Waterstones

IN THIS ISSUE

EDITOR'S LETTER

Dear Readers,
Celebrating our 40th issue is a milestone worth acknowledging, and The Reader's House is thrilled to continue being the voice of talented authors across the USA, UK, Canada, and beyond. Our commitment to supporting authors remains steadfast, and this issue is a testament to that dedication.

We're honored to feature the remarkable UK Crime Novelist, Sarah Hilary, whose work has captivated audiences worldwide. Her accolades, including winning the prestigious Theakston's Old Peculier Crime Novel of the Year award, speak volumes about the caliber of her writing. Sarah Hilary's DI Marnie Rome series, along with her standalone novels, exemplify the depth and brilliance present in crime fiction.

Moreover, our dedication to showcasing diverse voices is evident in the interviews conducted with a spectrum of talented authors in this issue. From Janice Hardy to Barbara Godin, from Susan Wiggs to Grace Allison Blair, Rina Brown, and Wayne Michael Hall, each conversation delves into their unique experiences and perspectives, enriching the literary landscape we aim to foster.

At The Reader's House, our mission is to celebrate the art of storytelling while providing a platform for both established and emerging authors. We take pride in presenting a mosaic of narratives that reflect the richness and diversity of voices in the literary world.

As we mark this significant edition, we extend our gratitude to our readers, contributors, and supporters. Your unwavering enthusiasm fuels our passion to continue championing authors and their stories. We're committed to further expanding our reach to feature more global talent, ensuring a tapestry of storytelling that resonates across borders.

As we approach the end of another year, we extend our warmest season's greetings to you. May this festive period be filled with joy, love, and cherished moments with your loved ones. Here's to a promising and prosperous new year ahead.

From all of us at The Reader's House, we wish you not only a Merry Christmas but also a season of self-discovery, self-care, and enriching reads. Thank you for being part of this incredible journey with us.

Fatih Oncu
Editor-in-Chief

PUBLISHER
The Reader's House
A Subsidiary of Newyox Media

200 Suite
134-146 Curtain Road
EC2A 3AR London
t: +44 79 3847 8420

editor@thereadershouse.co.uk
thereadershouse.com

EDITORIAL
Fatih Oncu
Editor-in-Chief
editor-in-chief@thereadershouse.co.uk
Anna Harlowe
editor@thereadershouse.co.uk
Dan Peters
dan.peters@thereadershouse.co.uk
Ben Alan
ben.alan@thereadershouse.co.uk

COVER PHOTO
Courtsey of Macmillan

CONTRIBUTOS
Claudine D. Reyes
Andrea Piacquadio
Adrian T. Cheng
Donna Schim
Jon Allo
Tim Halloran
Amir SeilSepour
Bill Youngblood
Jetty Stutzman
Jimmy Choo
Peter Filinovich
Rrodnae Productions

The Reader's House
thereadershouse.co.uk

Multi Award Winning, UK Crime Novelist

SARAH HILARY

Unraveling Complex Crime Narratives with Remarkable Depth

'An astonishingly gifted writer'
- Marian Keyes

BY FATIH ONCU

In the intricate world of crime fiction, Sarah Hilary stands as a beacon of excellence. With a debut novel that captured the prestigious Theakston's Old

"Sarah Hilary, award-winning crime novelist, shares literary passions, influences, and her unique approach to writing. Delving into character intricacies, inspirations, and a love for crime fiction's emotional landscapes.

Peculier Crime Novel of the Year Award and an ever-growing series featuring DI Marnie Rome, her storytelling prowess has garnered global recognition. Her second standalone novel, 'Black Thorn,' further cemented her reputation as a master of suspense.

However, beyond her own literary achievements, Sarah possesses an ardent passion for the works of others. In an exclusive interview, she unveils her deepest literary affections and shares the hidden gems that have left an indelible mark on her soul.

Her love for the written word transcends boundaries. Whether she's discussing the emotional suspense that captivates her or revealing her fascination with characters displaying quiet courage, Sarah's insights into the intricacies of literature are both profound and captivating.

As a writer herself, Sarah defies conventional advice, finding solace and inspiration in the pages of other authors' works while penning her own narratives. She delves into her childhood reading habits, highlighting the pivotal influence of iconic authors like Charlotte Brontë and Daphne du Maurier on her writing

journey.

Notably, Sarah's interview reveals her nuanced connection with characters who fall on the autistic spectrum, a reflection of her own identity and a commitment to representation in fiction.

From her admiration for Arthur Conan Doyle's iconic detec-

tive to her aspiration for her life story to be penned by a collaboration between Patricia Highsmith and Shirley Jackson, Sarah's reflections and desires are as intriguing as the gripping plots she crafts in her novels.

As she eagerly anticipates Megan Abbott's latest release as a

Continued *on page 10*

Notably, Sarah's interview reveals her nuanced connection with characters who fall on the autistic spectrum, a reflection of her own identity and a commitment to representation in fiction.

Continued *from page 8*

post-writing indulgence, Sarah Hilary remains a writer who not only crafts gripping tales of crime and suspense but also holds a profound appreciation for the power and beauty found within the written word.

Sarah Hilary's debut novel, Someone Else's Skin, won the 2015 Theakston's Old Peculier Crime Novel of the Year and was a World Book Night

"I would love Charlotte Brontë and Daphne du Maurier to come and talk about their lives and their books. The echoes of Jane Eyre in Rebecca have fascinated me since I was a child."

selection. The Observer's Book of the Month ('superbly disturbing') and a Richard and Judy Book Club bestseller, it has been published worldwide. No Other Darkness, the second in the series, was shortlisted for a Barry Award in the US. Her DI Marnie Rome series continues with Tastes Like Fear, Quieter Than Killing, Come and Find Me, and Never Be Broken. Black Thorn is her second standalone novel following Fragile.

What's your favorite book no one else has heard of?

A thriller called Sex Crimes by an American author, Jenefer Shute.

It's an extraordinary book, about a successful professional woman in her forties, who has what she intends to be a one-night stand with a younger man. This sparks the start of intense relationship that becomes increasingly obsessive – on his part as much as hers – and which ultimately ends in an appalling assault. The book opens with Christine in custody. She's been dubbed the Boston Fury by the media and no one, including her friends and family, can make sense of how she came to do the terrible thing for which she's standing trial. As the novel unfolds, Shute deploys her considerable skill as a storyteller to help us understand what happened and to illuminate what might happen next. I must have read and re-read Sex Crimes at least a dozen times, each time finding something new in it. The ending has haunted me for years. One of the most searingly truthful explorations of human frailty that I've ever read.

You're organizing a party. Which two authors, dead or alive, do you invite?

I would love Charlotte Brontë and Daphne du Maurier to come and

Sarah Hilary remains a writer who not only crafts gripping tales of crime and suspense but also holds a profound appreciation for the power and beauty found within the written word.

talk about their lives and their books. The echoes of Jane Eyre in Rebecca have fascinated me since I was a child. Both books were a huge source of inspiration when I was writing my first standalone thriller, Fragile. I'd ask Charlotte and Daphne their upbringings, their love of scaring themselves and their readers, their passion for landscape and escape … Each woman rebelled against her circumstances in different but similar ways. I'd want to talk about that. We'd eat soused mackerel from Fowey, and Yorkshire parkin. I'd try to be a good hostess and not just sit worshipping at their feet like a fangirl.

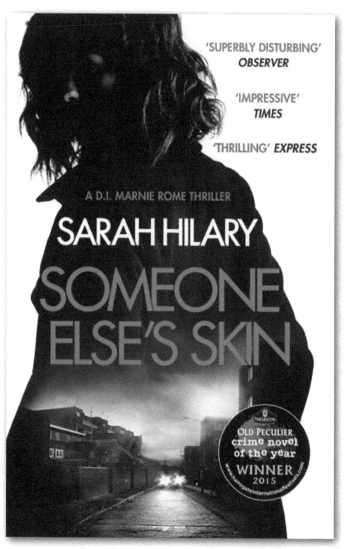

'SUPERBLY DISTURBING'
OBSERVER

'IMPRESSIVE'
TIMES

'THRILLING' **EXPRESS**

A D.I. MARNIE ROME THRILLER

SARAH HILARY

SOMEONE ELSE'S SKIN

OLD PECULIER crime novel of the year WINNER 2015

"Sarah Hilary's gripping novels, published by Macmillan, showcase the pinnacle of literary excellence, captivating readers worldwide with each thrilling narrative."

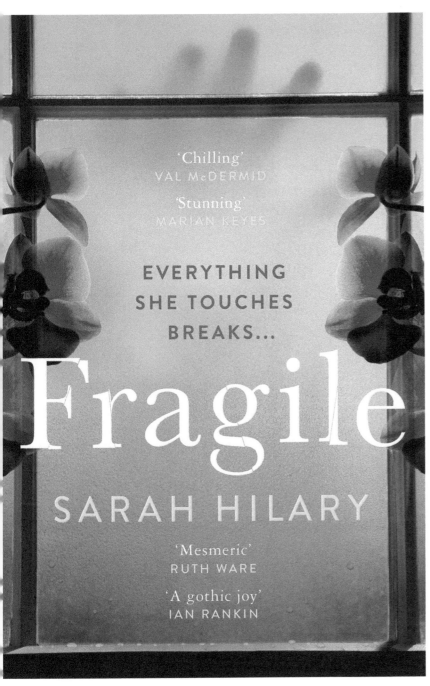

Fragile by Sarah Hilary

"Sarah Hilary's 'Fragile' is a haunting contemporary thriller filled with dark secrets and fractured lives. The story weaves a gripping narrative reminiscent of 'Rebecca' and 'The Handmaid's Tale,' showcasing the author's skill in crafting a chilling and psychologically intense tale. Hilary delivers a masterclass in modern Gothic fiction, drawing readers into a world where hidden pasts collide with uncertain futures, leaving an indelible mark on the psyche. A compelling, unsettling, and beautifully crafted standalone that reaffirms Hilary's place among top-tier psychological thriller writers."

What do you read when you're working on a book? And what kind of reading do you avoid while writing?

I read all the time, especially when I'm writing. Aspiring writers are often advised not to read fiction when writing but I honestly think this is the worst advice; books are what inspire us; it would be like telling a landscape artist not to go outside while working. I read fiction and non-fiction, finding that a combination of the two gives me the steer I need when I'm working on a new book. I also love short stories so will dip into those. I struggle to read poetry when I'm working, I suspect for the same reason I never listen to music when I'm writing – the rhythm of it gets in the way of the rhythms I'm trying to create in my own work.

What moves you most in a work of literature?

Always the emotional suspense. Like every crime writer, I love a puzzle but for me the real puzzles are people. I want to know what goes on inside their heads, what makes them tick. I'm moved by themes of loss and grief, and the idea of how cruelty or love can transform us in different ways. For me, true courage in a character isn't necessarily physical bravery or great feats of cunning or endurance. I'm moved by quiet courage, those small feats of determination that keep a character going against all odds. Jane Eyre is a good example of this kind of courage. One of my favourite French authors, Fred Vargas, created a hero called Jean-Baptiste Adamsberg who is quite possibly the quietest detective in all of crime fiction and, as a result, one of my favorites.

Who is your favorite fictional hero or heroine?

I have a very complicated relationship with my favorite fictional characters, and one which changes over time. When I first read Rebecca, I was eleven and in love with Maxim de Winter. Later, I fell for Rebecca herself, and also (more oddly) for Mrs Danvers. I do love both the young hero in My Cousin Rachel, and Rachel herself. The very first time I ever fell for a fictional hero and heroine, however, was when I read These Old Shades by Georgette Heyer at the age of ten. Leonie and her 'Monseigneur' are still two of my favourite characters in all of fiction.

I'm especially fond of characters who fall on the autistic spectrum, such as Patrick Fort in Rubbernecker by Belinda Bauer. I'm autistic myself, so I'm always looking out for characters with whom I can identify; there aren't nearly enough of them. In Black Thorn I created my first openly autistic heroine, in Agnes Gale. My detective, Noah Jake, in my D.I. Marnie Rome series was also autistic but I never used that word to describe him in the books. It was important to me to use the word autistic to describe Agnes in Black Thorn, as representa-

Continued *on page 12*

Continued *from page 11*

Find Sarah on X @Sarah_Hilary.

"Sarah Hilary's books are a symphony of suspense, weaving intricate mysteries around compelling characters. Each page is a labyrinth of secrets, exploring the darkest corners of human nature with raw emotion and depth. With a masterful blend of psychological depth and gripping narratives, her stories linger long after the final chapter ends."

tion in fiction really matters.

What kind of reader were you as a child?

Obsessive and a bit secretive ..! Books were my passion. Every summer, my mum would gift me two of her favourite novels from when she was the same age. This is how I came to read These Old Shades but also The Scarlet Pimpernel, A Dream of Sadler's Wells (and the other Lorna Hill ballet books), the ghost stories of MR James, Edgar Allan Poe, the Sherlock Holmes short stories and many, many more. When I was a teenager, my dad introduced me to Dick Francis and Raymond Chandler.

I also read comics (for girls and boys), and started writing my own books when I was about nine, including spy stories to entertain my little sister. I quickly developed my love of reading into a love of writing, partly because I wanted to make readers feel the way I felt when I was lost in a book.

If you could meet any writer, dead or alive, who would it be? And what would you want to know?

I'd quite like to ask Arthur Conan Doyle how he felt when his publisher insisted he resurrect Sherlock Holmes after he'd taken such trouble (and delight) in killing him off. I'd ask him when he

was first aware of hating this incredible character he'd created and how long it took him to come up with the plot to explain how Holmes survived that famous tumble into the Reichenbach Falls.

Which writer would you want to write your life story?

I'd love Patricia Highsmith and Shirley Jackson to collaborate to transform my story into something befitting a crime writer. I was lucky enough to have a very safe and happy childhood but that doesn't make for a gripping life story. In the hands of Highsmith and Jackson, I'm confident that I'd come across as a striking combination of Tom

Ripley and Merricat Blackwood. What more could a crime writer want ..?

What books do you find yourself returning to again and again?

As a writer, I'm intrigued by books that seem to shift and change over time. Rebecca is one example but also Red Dragon and Silence of the Lambs by Thomas Harris. I often re-read these to try and get a sense of how the author achieved this level of 'pull' for the reader, making me think about the characters long after the books are closed and put back on the shelf. As a reader, I'll return to favourites for reasons of comfort and nostalgia. I've

recently re-read my favourite thrillers by Mary Stewart, including Nine Coaches Waiting and The Ivy Tree.

What do you plan to read next?

I've been promising myself Megan Abbott's new novel, Beware the Woman, as a treat for when I've finished writing my next book. Megan is one of my favourite writers, a source of real inspiration. She writes particularly well about the emotional landscapes in our hearts and minds, taking us into the darkest corners and shedding her own brand of light on what we find there ●

WINTER SKIN SURVIVAL GUIDE: EXPERT TIPS FOR YEAR-ROUND RADIANCE

Winter demands ongoing skin protection. Exposure to indoor and outdoor elements can harm skin health. Dermatologist Rachel Nazarian advises year-round SPF use, supplements like Heliocare for antioxidants, device limitation, and quality sleep for optimal skin repair and health.

PHOTO: Embracing Winter Radiance: Keeping skin healthy with expert tips from dermatologist Rachel Nazarian for a glowing, year-round complexion.

Photo by Chris Cross / iStock via Getty Images Plus

If you're like many people, you may view the change in seasons as a sign that you can give up your skin protection routine. Experts say that everyone, regardless of gender or lifestyle, should be careful not to neglect their skin health in winter.

"Don't let your guard down in winter. Not only are you still being exposed to sunlight and pollution during these colder months, but there are sources of free radicals indoors, too, which may have negative, aging effects on the skin. Free radicals can damage the skin's cell function and DNA, and DNA changes can cause mutations that could increase the risk of skin cancer," says New York City dermatologist, Rachel Nazarian, MD FAAD.

To invest in your skin health this winter, and all year long, Dr. Nazarian offers the following tips:

• Keep up the SPF routine: Don't stow that bottle of sunscreen away. Applying a topical broad spectrum SPF on a daily basis can protect skin while you're enjoying time outdoors, and from the incidental exposure that occurs through a window indoors, like while driving.

• Get inside-out protection: While topical protection is important, ultimate skin health requires a combination of defensive layers. Amp up your skin protection routine with a daily supplement, such as Heliocare. Clinically proven and recommended by 87% of U.S. dermatologists surveyed, this vegan and gluten-free natural dietary supplement has antioxidant effects on the skin and contains Fernblock PLE Technology, a proprietary ingredient that aids in neutralizing the negative effects of free radicals.

"Whether you're a ski bunny or prefer hibernating all winter, there is no time of year when your skin is immune to free radical damage. A popular skin concern, collagen loss, can create signs of aging, like wrinkling, fine-lines and sagging. Since collagen loss is expedited by free radical damage, taking a supplement like Heliocare all year long is an excellent precaution to help your body protect itself from the damaging effects of free radicals ," says Dr. Nazarian.

To learn more, visit heliocare.com.

• Put the device down: Protect your skin from excessive exposure to the visible light emitted from digital screens like cellphones and laptops. To do so, find small, easy ways to limit your device usage, such as reading a physical book instead of using an e-reader, or by playing records instead of playing DJ on your phone. You can also reduce exposure by simply turning the brightness down on your devices.

• Sleep tight: During sleep, your body works to repair organs, including your skin. Getting high-quality, deep sleep each night is essential for healthy skin and a healthy body. According to The Sleep Foundation, the best temperature for sleep is 65 degrees Fahrenheit, even in winter when it's tempting to turn up the thermostat to toastier temperatures. You can also promote good sleep by keeping alcohol and caffeine consumption in check, and by turning to sleep apps that soothe users into slumber with meditation and white noise.

To help keep skin healthy and radiant, don't neglect it in the winter months. For best results, ensure your care routine is both comprehensive, and year-round.

Protecting Your Skin Year-Round: Winter Tips for Radiant Health" offers insights from dermatologist Rachel Nazarian on maintaining skin health during winter. Emphasizing the importance of SPF, supplements like Heliocare, minimizing digital screen exposure, and prioritizing quality sleep, it advocates a comprehensive, year-round care routine for glowing skin.

JANICE HARDY
Crafting Worlds, Inspiring Minds

Janice Hardy, a diverse writer and mentor, shares her eclectic reading tastes, influences, and the magic of storytelling, guiding writers through Fiction University's embrace.

Janice Hardy, the mastermind behind captivating tales of adventure, is a force to be reckoned with in the literary world. Known for her belief that subjecting her characters to trials enhances their allure, she has seamlessly navigated the realms of both young adult fiction and adult novels. Under the pseudonym J.T. Hardy, she delves into the more mature spheres of storytelling, demonstrating her versatility and depth as a writer. Beyond her fictional endeavors, Hardy is a guiding beacon for aspiring writers through her non-fiction work, aiding them in honing their craft and navigating the labyrinthine landscape of publishing. Her brainchild, Fiction University, serves as a haven for writers seeking guidance and insight.

In a candid conversation with The Reader's House magazine, Hardy revealed facets of her literary persona that illuminate her as both a reader and a writer. Her eclectic taste in literature spans across genres and eras, reflecting a voracious appetite for stories that captivate and resonate on multiple levels.

One intriguing revelation from the interview was Hardy's penchant for Diane Setterfield's "The Thirteenth Tale." Despite Setterfield's acclaim in literary circles, this particular novel remains a hidden gem within Hardy's preferred genres. The allure of an enigmatic author weaving an ever-evolving life narrative captivated Hardy, showcasing her penchant for narratives that transcend conventional storytelling boundaries.

Hardy's admiration extends to contemporary writers, particularly romance authors, whom she regards as among the most hardworking and business-savvy in the industry. Her admiration for Tiffany Reisz's prolific output and storytelling prowess highlights Hardy's appreciation for dedication and skill in crafting engaging narratives.

When asked about her favorite writers, Hardy listed luminaries such as Harlan Ellison, John Scalzi, Ilona Andrews, Jennifer Crusie, and Angela Quarles. Her en-

dorsement of these authors extends beyond mere admiration; they are her "auto-buy" favorites, a testament to their ability to consistently deliver compelling reads. She also reminisced about childhood favorites like Walter Farley, whose "Black Stallion" series left an indelible mark on her literary journey.

For Hardy, reading and writing are symbiotic processes. While she once avoided reading within the genre she was writing to prevent influence, she now finds solace and inspiration in diverse genres. Her reading choices vary based on mood, opting for lighter fare during intense writing phases and delving into deeper, immersive narratives during clearer, focused periods.

The impact of various authors on Hardy's career is evident. Harlan Ellison's enthralling storytelling ignited her passion for crafting engaging narratives, while Dave Duncan and Holly Lisle's works served as guiding lights, inspiring her to dissect their writing styles and learn from their voices.

Her childhood was marked by an insatiable appetite for reading and writing. Hardy's voracious reading habits often outpaced her classmates, leading her to indulge in writing her own stories from an early age. Her literary curiosity and creative drive were evident even then, culminating in the completion of her first novel at the tender age of twelve.

In her personal literary repertoire, certain books hold a perennial place. Jennifer Crusie's works, including "Anyone but You" and "Agnes and the Hitman," are seasonal re-reads for Hardy, providing a sense of comfort and familiarity. Additionally, Max Brooks's "World War Z" and Ilona Andrews's series like "Kate Daniels" and "Innkeeper" resonate deeply with her, inviting periodic revisits into their immersive worlds.

Janice Hardy's literary journey is a testament to her multifaceted talent and unwavering passion for storytelling. Her eclectic tastes, admiration for fellow writers, and commitment to nurturing aspiring authors through Fiction University cement her position as a luminary in the literary landscape. Hardy's ability to spin tales that resonate across age groups and genres is a testament to her prowess as a storyteller and an inspiration to both readers and aspiring writers alike.

PHOTO: *Janice Hardy, the prolific author behind captivating tales of adventure and guidance for aspiring writers through Fiction University.*

New Book

A Demon's Guide to Wooing a Witch

By Sarah Hawley
Category: Contemporary Romance

Magic clashes with a fiery witch's rage when she aids an amnesiac demon. Their journey sparks unexpected chemistry, challenging prejudices in a spellbinding tale of redemption and love.

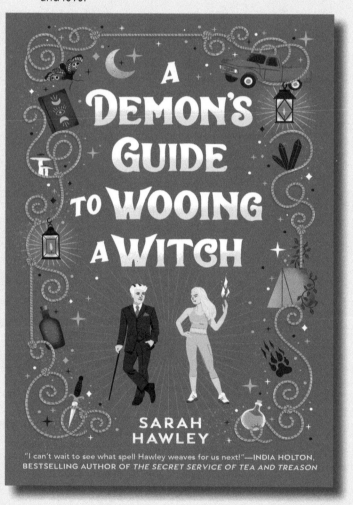

"A Demon's Guide to Wooing a Witch" by Sarah Hawley: Heiress Calladia reluctantly aids amnesiac demon Astaroth against a common foe. Their journey unveils unexpected connections, blending magic, redemption, and a captivating, evolving romance.

A Demon's Guide to Wooing a Witch" by Sarah Hawley is a captivating tale blending magic, redemption, and unexpected chemistry. Calladia Cunnington, heir to a witch family in Glimmer Falls, has a fiery temperament that often lands her in bar brawls. However, when she saves a helpless amnesiac from a demon attack, she's shocked to discover it's none other than Astaroth, the demon behind a soul bargain that affected her best friend.

Astaroth, a renowned soul bargainer and a member of the demon high council, finds himself on Earth with no memory of his past. As Calladia reluctantly agrees to help him navigate his amnesia, their journey begins. Despite her initial animosity, she discovers a different side to Astaroth, his charm slowly eroding her disdain.

Their uneasy alliance takes them on a road trip in search of a witch capable of restoring Astaroth's memories, all while evading the threats posed by Moloch, a menacing presence hunting him down. As their journey progresses, Calladia grapples with conflicting emotions. The more she grows fond of the reformed Astaroth, the less she desires his memories to return.

Hawley weaves a tale that balances tension and allure, drawing readers into a world where magic intertwines with complex emotions. The dynamic between Calladia and Astaroth is magnetic, evolving from hostility to an unexpected connection that challenges their initial perceptions.

The story navigates themes of redemption, forgiveness, and the complexities of identity, unraveling the layers of both characters as they confront their pasts. Hawley skillfully crafts a narrative that keeps readers engaged, rooting for the characters' growth and the unearthing of their intertwined destinies.

"A Demon's Guide to Wooing a Witch" is a spellbinding romance brimming with humor, magic, and the exploration of second chances—a delightful read for fans of enchanting love stories set against a backdrop of supernatural intrigue.

Fear of Flying

50TH ANNIVERSARY EDITION
By Erica Jong

Foreword by Molly Jong-Fast
Introduction by Taffy

Brodesser-Akner

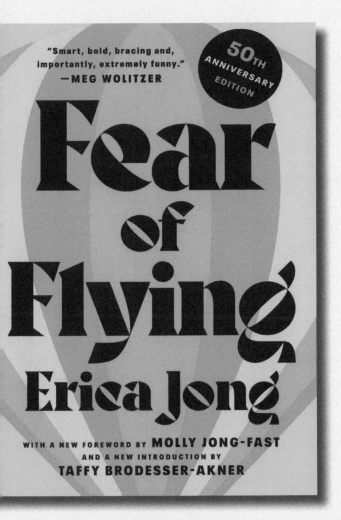

"Fear of Flying" follows Isadora Wing's quest for fulfillment beyond societal norms, evolving from a pursuit of no-strings-attached sex to a profound journey of self-discovery and female liberation.

Originally published in 1973, Erica Jong's daring narrative challenges taboos, exploring desires, fears, and complexities of womanhood with wit and candor. The book remains a timeless reflection on autonomy and the pursuit of personal aspirations.

Fear of Flying" is a groundbreaking exploration of Isadora Wing's quest for freedom amidst societal constraints. Originally published in 1973, this daring novel by Erica Jong continues to resonate as a timeless journey of self-discovery and female empowerment.

Isadora, disillusioned with her life, embarks on a search for fulfillment beyond societal norms. Her pursuit of sexual liberation unfolds into a deeper exploration of her desires, fears, and the complexities of womanhood. The narrative challenges taboos, sparking both admiration and controversy for its candid portrayal of female desires and relationships.

Jong's writing is smart, daring, and laced with humor, inviting readers into Isadora's unapologetic and introspective world. The book remains a poignant reflection on the struggle for autonomy and the pursuit of one's true aspirations.

"Fear of Flying" remains a literary milestone that broke barriers and continues to inspire discussions about sexuality, identity, and the pursuit of personal freedom. Fifty years on, its relevance endures, making it an enduring testament to self-discovery and the ongoing journey toward empowerment.

The Boardwalk Bookshop

By Susan Mallery

Susan Mallery's "The Boardwalk Bookshop" weaves a tale of three women finding solace and strength in friendship amid personal struggles. Set in a charming California space, their bond deepens, navigating betrayals, divorce, and the pursuit of love, culminating in a heartwarming journey of self-discovery and resilience.

S usan Mallery's "The Boardwalk Bookshop" unveils a captivating narrative cocooned within the essence of friendship, resilience, and the allure of new beginnings. Set against the picturesque California coast, the tale follows the intertwining lives of three women brought together by fate and united by their entrepreneurial dreams.

Bree, Mikki, and Ashley, the dynamic trio behind the Boardwalk Bookshop, converge in a shared space that embodies their aspirations—a haven blending bookstore, gift shop, and bakery. As their professional endeavors flourish, their personal lives spiral in tumultuous directions, each grappling with uncharted emotional territories.

Mallery artfully sketches each protagonist's intricate backstory, layering their lives with depth and authenticity. Bree, haunted by a past scarred by betrayal, guards her heart behind impenetrable walls until Ashley's brother nudges past her defenses, unsettling her guarded equilibrium. Mikki, navigating the complexities of divorce with an uncanny ease, finds her world upended by an unexpected romantic entanglement, challenging her perceptions of herself.

The allure of Mallery's storytelling lies not just in the characters' individual struggles, but in the collective strength they find within their blossoming friendship. Each Friday, against the backdrop of a sun-kissed beach, these women share moments of camaraderie and solace, embracing the transformative power of their bond. Through shared toasts and heartfelt conversations, they inspire and uplift one another, catalyzing a profound journey of self-discovery and growth.

The narrative's resonance lies in its portrayal of human vulnerabilities and the healing balm of connection. Mallery deftly explores themes of love, self-acceptance, and the pursuit of happiness, anchoring her tale in the nuances of sisterhood and the inherent strength derived from female solidarity.

"The Boardwalk Bookshop" radiates warmth and authenticity, drawing readers into a world where friendships burgeon against life's unpredictable backdrop. Mallery's narrative prowess shines through in her ability to craft a story that is at once poignant and hopeful, celebrating the resilience of the human spirit.

In this heartachingly beautiful story, Mallery crafts a tale that is both a celebration of friendship's power and an ode to the transformative nature of love. "The Boardwalk Bookshop" beckons readers into a world where personal journeys intertwine, leading to a symphony of self-discovery and the enchanting allure of new beginnings.

#1 *New York Times* Bestselling Author

SUSAN MALLERY

THE BOARDWALK BOOKSHOP

"Dive into the enchanting world of 'The Boardwalk Bookshop' by Susan Mallery—a tale of friendship, resilience, and the transformative power of love. A perfect companion for cozy reading moments."

"Susan Mallery's 'The Boardwalk Bookshop' is a heartwarming masterpiece! With rich characters, evocative settings, and an emotionally resonant storyline, Mallery crafts a narrative that celebrates the enduring strength of friendship and the beauty of new beginnings. A must-read!"

- The Reader's House

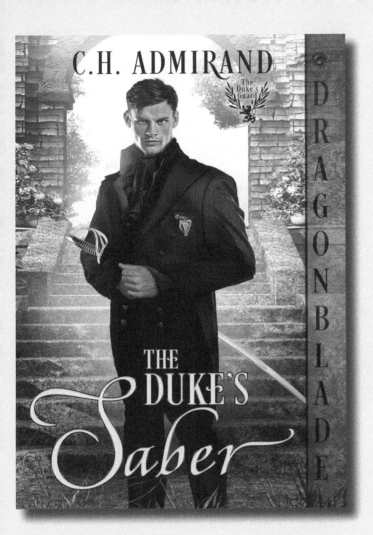

The Duke's Saber
by C.H. Admirand

"The Duke's Saber"
by C.H. Admirand:
A tale of duty and unexpected
love as Ryan, a steadfast Saber,
navigates loyalty, danger, and
blossoming affection with
Prudence amid perilous
circumstances.

In "The Duke's Saber," C.H. Admirand crafts a riveting tale woven with a tapestry of duty, honor, and the allure of unexpected love. Set against the backdrop of a time when loyalty was paramount, this novel transports readers to an era where the protection of a noble family requires not only courage but also a heart unyielding in its devotion.

At the center of this captivating narrative is Ryan Garahan, a stalwart member of the Duke of Wyndmere's elite Saber. Admirand skillfully portrays Ryan's unwavering commitment to his duty, shaping him as a figure of unwavering strength and resolve. His dedication to safeguarding the Duke's family is unwavering, a quality that echoes through every page with resounding loyalty.

However, fate's whims challenge Ryan's staunch allegiance when he encounters Prudence Barstow, the governess entrusted with the safety of her young twin cousins. Their meeting sparks a series of events that test Ryan's steadfastness, as he finds himself not only drawn to Prudence's spirited nature but also ensnared by her undeniable charm. Admirand expertly navigates the complexities of their burgeoning connection, deftly entwining it with the looming threat that shadows their every step.

The author masterfully paints a vivid picture of the Borderlands, a setting rich with lush landscapes and looming dangers. From the ancient oaks to the serene ponds, each scene is meticulously crafted, evoking a sense of immersive authenticity that envelops readers in its ambiance.

Amidst the palpable danger lurking in the shadows, the narrative unfolds with a compelling rhythm, seamlessly blending moments of heart-pounding suspense with tender interludes of burgeoning affection. Admirand's prose effortlessly captures the essence of each character, endowing them with depth and authenticity that resonate throughout the tale.

The chemistry between Ryan and Prudence is electrifying, their interactions brimming with palpable tension and undeniable chemistry. Their dynamic unfolds in a dance of emotions, drawing readers into a captivating romance that blossoms amidst the challenges they face.

"The Duke's Saber" stands as a testament to Admirand's storytelling prowess, showcasing her ability to intertwine passion, honor, and peril in a narrative that grips the reader from the very first page. With meticulous attention to detail and a narrative that pulsates with emotion, this book is a testament to the power of duty and the resilience of love.

Praise for "The Duke's Saber":

C.H. Admirand's "The Duke's Saber" is a tour de force in historical romance. With a deft hand, Admirand crafts a tale brimming with intrigue, passion, and unwavering devotion. The characters leap off the pages, each one meticulously sculpted with depth and nuance that captivate the reader's imagination.

Ryan Garahan's portrayal as a protector bound by duty and honor is nothing short of mesmerizing. His unwavering commitment to the Duke's family is a testament to Admirand's ability to create characters that resonate on a profound level. Prudence Barstow, the governess whose spirited nature and undeniable charm captivate both Ryan and readers alike, is a beacon of strength amidst the encroaching dangers of the Borderlands.

Admirand's vivid descriptions transport readers to a world teeming with lush landscapes and imminent peril, creating an immersive experience that lingers long after the final page is turned. The chemistry between Ryan and Prudence crackles with intensity, their interactions a delightful blend of tension and tenderness.

"The Duke's Saber" is a triumph—a tale that seamlessly weaves together passion, honor, and danger. Admirand's narrative prowess shines through, delivering a story that resonates with emotion and authenticity. For fans of historical romance, this book is an absolute must-read—a captivating journey that ensnares the heart and soul.

New & Noteworthy

PAX

By Sara Pennypacker, Illustrated by Jon Klassen

New York Times Bestseller * National Book Award Longlist

Finally in paperback! This handsome edition features French flaps.

From bestselling and award-winning author Sara Pennypacker comes a beautifully wrought, utterly compelling novel about the powerful relationship between a boy and his fox. Pax is destined to become a classic, beloved for generations to come.

Pax and Peter have been inseparable ever since Peter rescued him as a kit. But one day, the unimaginable happens: Peter's dad enlists in the military and makes him return the fox to the wild.

At his grandfather's house, three hundred miles away from home, Peter knows he isn't where he should be—with Pax. He strikes out on his own despite the encroaching war, spurred by love, loyalty, and grief, to be reunited with his fox.

Meanwhile Pax, steadfastly waiting for his boy, embarks on adventures and discoveries of his own. . . .

Pax is a wonderful choice for independent reading, sharing in the classroom, homeschooling, and book groups.

Plus, don't miss Pax, Journey Home, the sequel to the award-winning and modern classic Pax.

The Night Watchman
Pulitzer Prize Winning Fiction
By Louise Erdrich

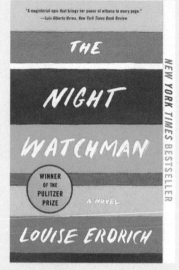

NEW YORK TIMES BESTSELLER

WASHINGTON POST, NPR, CBS SUNDAY MORNING, KIRKUS, CHICAGO PUBLIC LIBRARY, AND GOOD HOUSEKEEPING BEST BOOK OF THE YEAR

Based on the extraordinary life of National Book Award-winning author Louise Erdrich's grandfather who worked as a night watchman and carried the fight against Native dispossession from rural North Dakota all the way to Washington, D.C., this powerful novel explores themes of love and death with lightness and gravity and unfolds with the elegant prose, sly humor, and depth of feeling of a master craftsman.

Thomas Wazhashk is the night watchman at the jewel bearing plant, the first factory located near the Turtle Mountain Reservation in rural North Dakota. He is also a Chippewa Council member who is trying to understand the consequences of a new "emancipation" bill on its way to the floor of the United States Congress. It is 1953 and he and the other council members know the bill isn't about freedom; Congress is fed up with Indians. The bill is a "termination" that threatens the rights of Native Americans to their land and their very identity. How can the government abandon treaties made in good faith with Native Americans "for as long as the grasses shall grow, and the rivers run"?

Since graduating high school, Pixie Paranteau has insisted that everyone call her Patrice. Unlike most of the girls on the reservation, Patrice, the class valedictorian, has no desire to wear herself down with a husband and kids. She makes jewel bearings at the plant, a job that barely pays her enough to support her mother and brother. Patrice's shameful alcoholic father returns home sporadically to terrorize his wife and children and bully her for money. But Patrice needs every penny to follow her beloved older sister, Vera, who moved to the big city of Minneapolis. Vera may have disappeared; she hasn't been in touch in months, and is rumored to have had a baby. Determined to find Vera and her child, Patrice makes a fateful trip to Minnesota that introduces her to unexpected forms of exploitation and violence, and endangers her life.

Thomas and Patrice live in this impoverished reservation community along with young Chippewa boxer Wood Mountain and his mother Juggie Blue, her niece and Patrice's best friend Valentine, and Stack Barnes, the white high school math teacher and boxing coach who is hopelessly in love with Patrice.

In the Night Watchman, Louise Erdrich creates a fictional world populated with memorable characters who are forced to grapple with the worst and best impulses of human nature. Illuminating the loves and lives, the desires and ambitions of these characters with compassion, wit, and intelligence, The Night Watchman is a majestic work of fiction from this revered cultural treasure.

Travelers to Unimaginable Lands

STORIES OF DEMENTIA, THE CAREGIVER, AND THE HUMAN BRAIN

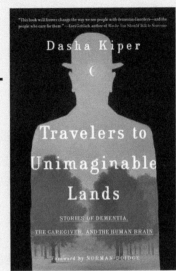

By Dasha Kiper
Foreword by Norman Doidge
Category: Psychology | Health & Fitness

These compelling case histories meld science and storytelling to illuminate the complex relationship between the mind of someone with dementia and the mind of the person caring for them.

"This book will forever change the way we see people with dementia disorders—and the people who care for them."—Lori Gottlieb, author of Maybe You Should Talk to Someone

After getting a master's degree in clinical psychology, Dasha Kiper became the live-in caregiver for a Holocaust survivor with Alzheimer's disease. For a year, she endured the emotional strain of looking after a person whose condition disrupts the rules of time, order, and continuity. Inspired by her own experience and her work counseling caregivers in the subsequent decade, Kiper offers an entirely new way to understand the symbiotic relationship between patients and those tending to them. Her book is the first to examine how the workings of the "healthy" brain prevent us from adapting to and truly understanding the cognitively impaired one.

In these poignant but unsentimental stories of parents and children, husbands and wives, Kiper explores the existential dilemmas created by this disease: A man believes his wife is an impostor. A woman's imaginary friendships drive a wedge between herself and her devoted husband. Another woman's childhood trauma emerges to torment her son. A man's sudden Catholic piety provokes his wife.

Why is taking care of a family member with dementia so difficult? Why do caregivers succumb to behaviors—arguing, blaming, insisting, taking symptoms personally—they know are counterproductive? Exploring the healthy brain's intuitions and proclivities, Travelers to Unimaginable Lands reveals the neurological obstacles to caregiving, enumerating not only the terrible pressures the disease exerts on our closest relationships but offering solace and perspective as well.

New & Noteworthy

What Is the Story of Captain Picard?

By David Stabler and Who HQ
Illustrated by Robert Squier

Category: Childrens Media Tie-In Books | Children's Middle Grade Books

Your favorite characters are now part of the Who HQ library!

Climb aboard the starship USS Enterprise and learn how Jean-Luc Picard became one of the most beloved Starfleet members in the Star Trek universe.

Star Trek stands as one of the most popular science-fiction series of all time, and Captain Picard is one of its fan-favorite characters thanks to his inspiring quotes and brilliant leadership. As the captain of the starship USS Enterprise, Picard has taken viewers with him on adventures through space for decades. Now, young fans can learn even more about the famous character, including details about his obsessions with Earl Grey tea and Shakespeare.

From appearances in live-action and animated television shows, a series of films, comics, video games, and more, Jean-Luc Picard is an established icon in the Star Trek universe and a beloved character across pop-culture channels.

Author David Stabler takes readers aboard Starfleet starships as Picard adventures through space, defeats great evils, and inspires hope in us all to believe that "things are only impossible until they're not."

UNVEILING TRUTHS

Navigating Life's Depths through Words, Wisdom, and Resilience

A conversation with
BARBARA GODIN

Barbara Godin weaves poignant narratives that resonate deeply, showcasing resilience in her memoir "Can I Come HOME Now?" Her "Dear Barb" series offers insightful advice on everyday challenges. With a skillful touch, Godin's writing unveils raw emotions and invites readers on transformative journeys. Explore her compelling works at barbgodin.com.

Barbara Godin received her B.A. from Athabasca University, Edmonton, Alberta Canada. She began writing her popular "Dear Barb" column in 2003. In 2019 Barbara won the first-place award in a short article contest from the prestigious Professional Writers Association of Canada (PWAC) for "Mary's Story."

Barbara is the author of five books. "Dear Barb: Answers to Your Everyday Questions" "Glimpses in Time: A Collection of Memoirs and More" also "Dear Barb 2: Advice for Daily Life" and her bestselling memoir "Can I Come HOME Now?" Barbara's latest book "Seasons of the Heart" is a collection of poetry.

Barbara was born in Windsor Ontario Canada. She now resides in Chatham Ontario Canada with her husband and their ginger cat aptly named "Prince Harry.

barbgod   X   BarbGod   f   https://barbgodin.com/

"In the pages of 'Can I Come HOME Now?' Barbara Godin bravely unveils the echoes of her past, offering a poignant tool for healing and a voice for those silenced by abuse."

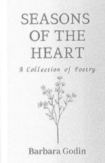

Explore worlds within words. Discover Barbara Godin's captivating stories that transport you to places unseen and emotions untold. Dive into her books for a journey unlike any other.

"Within every page, Barbara Godin weaves tapestries of imagination, inviting us to wander through worlds unseen, emotions unspoken, and stories that resonate deeply within."

What is the last great book you read?

The last book I read was "The True Story of Canadian Human Trafficking" by Paul H. Boge. It was a difficult read, but a story that needed to be told. I had no idea this was going on in Canada to the extent that it is. The author was very thorough and included all sides of the issue.

If you organising a party who would you invite?

I were organizing a party I would invite Tara Westover and Maya Angelou. I enjoyed Tara Westover's memoir "Educated" and Maya Angelou has written seven autobiographies. I believe her most famous memoir is "I Know Why the Caged Bird Sings."

Which writers working today do you admire the most?

I admire Ryan Green's ability to write true crime and I truly enjoyed "The Midwife of Auschwitz" by Anna Stuart, although it was a difficult book to absorb.

What do you read when you're working on a book? And what kind of reading do you avoid?

When I am working on a book I read books that are similar to the genre I am writing. I avoid books that will be too engulfing and distract me from writing.

What genre do you enjoy reading?

I enjoy reading autobiographies, memoirs, and poetry.

What kind of books do your family and friends read?

My family and friends read mostly nonfiction, true crime, and memoirs. My husband reads strictly fiction.

What first piqued your interest in reading when you were a child?

As a child, I spent one year living with my father and he often took me out on Friday nights and bought me two or three books. I always made sure I read the books before I got new ones.

When did you begin writing?

My life was very difficult and keeping a journal helped me to cope with some of the abuse and neglect I experienced while growing up.

Which book is your most popular book and why?

My most popular book is my memoir "Can I Come HOME Now?" It is most popular because of the horrific abuse I experienced. My book is a tool for many families to discuss abuse that may have occurred within their own family but have never been able to discuss.

Which book do you wish was more popular?

I wish my "Dear Barb" series was more popular. I feel it contains a lot of interesting advice about everyday issues, that everyone can benefit from.

PHOTO: *The #1 New York Times bestselling author brings us her most ambitious and provocative work yet—a searing and timely novel that explores the most volatile issue of our time— domestic violence—and the sustaining power of women's friendships.*

A Journey of Love, Family, and Fiction

SUSAN WIGGS

#1 New York Times Best Seller Author

Susan Wiggs, the celebrated and #1 New York Times Best Seller author, draws inspiration from her Puget Sound island home, crafting novels that celebrate love, family, and human nature. With millions of copies of her books in print worldwide, she's known for her honest emotion and unforgettable storytelling. Her literary journey reflects her lifelong love for reading and diverse influences, making her a beacon in the literary world.

By Anna Harlowe

Susan Wiggs, #1 New York Times Best Seller Author is a name that resonates with lovers of contemporary fiction. Her life, like her novels, is a tapestry of family, friends, and a deep connection to the world around her. In this article, we delve into the life and literary journey of Susan Wiggs, a renowned international best-selling author who has touched the hearts of readers all over the world.

A Life by the Water

Susan Wiggs's life is intimately tied to the natural beauty of Puget Sound. She resides on an island in this picturesque part of the world, where the ebb and flow of the water serve as both inspiration and solace. It's

no wonder that her storytelling often draws from the landscapes that surround her. In fair weather, she even commutes to her writers' group in a 21-foot motorboat, underlining her deep connection to the sea.

The serene setting of her home is not just a place to rest her head; it's a muse that infuses her novels with a sense of place and authenticity. Wiggs's writing beautifully captures the essence of the Pacific Northwest, a place where everyday people navigate extraordinary circumstances, and where the bonds of love and family hold an enduring power.

A Literary Journey

Wiggs's literary journey began with a focus on the everyday dramas of ordinary people. Her

Susan Wiggs has created a literary legacy that continues to grow and captivate readers worldwide. Her ability to craft stories that touch the heart and illuminate the everyday struggles of ordinary people is a testament to her talent.

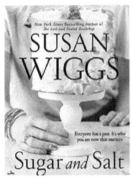

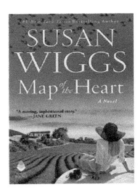

25 million copies in print. Published in 30 countries. Translated into over 20 languages. To say that #1 NYT bestselling author Susan Wiggs is an accomplished writer would be nothing short of an understatement. A Harvard graduate and former math teacher, Susan's passion for writing dates back to grade school when she penned her first book, titled A Book About Some Bad Kids.

novels are a celebration of the profound impact of love, the enduring strength of familial ties, and the complex intricacies of human nature. Her ability to portray these elements with honesty and depth has garnered her a dedicated readership.

Her books have been published in numerous countries and translated into various languages, making her a truly international author. With millions of copies of her books in print, her impact on the world of fiction is undeniable. Publishers Weekly commends her for writing with "refreshingly honest emotion," and the Salem Statesman Journal notes that she is "one of our best observers of stories of the heart," capturing emotion on every page of every book. Booklist characterizes her novels as "real and true and unforgettable."

A Life Beyond Writing

Susan Wiggs is not just a talented writer; she is a woman of diverse interests and talents. She has a background in education and is a Harvard graduate, demonstrating her commitment to intellectual pursuits. Her love for the outdoors is evident in her passion for hiking and amateur photography. While she may be a self-proclaimed terrible golfer, she's an avid skier and, most importantly, an ardent reader.

Wiggs's favourite form of exercise is not found in physical activity but in the solace of a good book. Her love for literature is evident in her writing, where she weaves intricate stories that captivate the hearts and minds of her readers.

Inspirations and Influences

Every writer is shaped by the books they read, and Susan Wiggs is no exception. She draws inspiration from a wide range of authors and texts that have influenced her writing journey. When asked about the last great book she read, she mentions "The Heart's Invisible Furies" by John Boyne, a coming-of-age story that covers a man's life, describing it as both heart-breaking and uplifting.

She also has a fondness for "Avalon" by Anya Seton, which may not be widely recognized but is a treasure among those who appreciate Seton's work. This particular book offers Seton's interpretation of the Arthurian legends.

Her favourite fictional hero or heroine is Celie from Alice Walker's "The Colour Purple." Celie embodies resilience and strength, qualities that resonate with Wiggs and are often reflected in her own characters.

As for the books and authors that have impacted her writing career, Wiggs cites several influential titles. "Techniques of the Selling Writer" by Dwight Swain, "The Writer's Journey" by Christopher Vogler, "Writing the Breakout Novel" by Donald Maass, and "Writing Fiction" by Janet Burroway have all played a significant role in shaping her craft.

The Young Reader

Susan Wiggs's lifelong love for reading had its roots in her childhood. She was a voracious reader, devouring everything she could get her hands on. Her reading repertoire included a full set of encyclopaedias, and she even set herself the ambitious task of reading a biography for each letter of the alphabet during one summer.

As a middle child, Susan Wiggs had a penchant for mischief, but her other defining trait was her insatiable appetite for books.

She read series books, classic novels, and virtually anything she could find. Her childhood as a reader laid the foundation for her future as a writer, as her early experiences with literature allowed her to explore diverse worlds and characters.

A Beacon in the Literary World

Susan Wiggs has created a literary legacy that continues to grow and captivate readers worldwide. Her ability to craft stories that touch the heart and illuminate the everyday struggles of ordinary people is a testament to her talent. With a deep appreciation for the power of love, family, and the intricate workings of the human soul, she has cemented her place as an international best-selling author.

As her readers immerse themselves in her novels, they embark on journeys filled with emotion, authenticity, and unforgettable storytelling. Whether you're navigating the intricate waters of Puget Sound or curling up with one of Susan Wiggs's books, you're sure to find a sense of connection and a deep appreciation for the beauty of love and life's everyday dramas.

PHOTO: *Rodney Bond and his wife with their son*

JOURNEYS THROUGH UNIVERSES

Navigating Life's Depths through Words, Wisdom, and Resilience

A conversation with
RODNEY BOND

"Rodney Bond, an engineer turned award-winning teacher, explored genealogy, wrote diverse books, and valued historical and scientific complexity. His favorite characters and interests span literature, science fiction, and history."

R odney Bond has a B.S. in Aerospace Engineering and an M.S. in Computer Science. Rodney first served in the Air Force as a B-52D navigator/bombardier, then as an engineer in the defense industry. In his mid-forties, Rodney became a high school teacher in Texas. Rodney coached students to state championships in science and mathematics. In 2010, Rodney was named the MIT High School Inspirational Teacher of the Year. In 2011, Rodney was selected as a Claes Nobel Educator of Distinction. During these years, Rodney did genealogical research, which he documented on his website, "Many Mini Biographies." The website has over one million hits. Upon retiring, Rodney began writing books on various subjects.

"Science and God"

The book explores multiple universes, inspired by science and philosophy. It delves into individual experiences shaping unique realities, challenging predictable physics and celebrating life's unpredictable elements.

"Exploring Parallel Realities, Lifelong Learning, and the Power of Individual Universes"

Rodney Bond, an aerospace engineer turned high school teacher, achieved success in coaching students to state championships. With expertise in genealogy and over a million hits on his website, he later authored books spanning history, science, and the Bible. Bond's favorite fictional hero is "Honor Harrington," and he would invite Isaac Asimov and Frank Herbert to a literary party.

Who is your favorite fictional hero or heroine?

"Honor Harrington" of the series by David Weber.

You're organizing a party. Which two authors, dead or alive, do you invite?

Issac Asimov for the Foundation series, and Frank Herbert for the Dune series.

What moves you most in a work of literature?

The complexities of the plot and the scope of the story.

What genres do you especially enjoy reading?

Multi-book series, especially science fiction, fantasy, and mystery, with recurring characters.

What kind of reader were you as a child?

At an early age I favored comic books. I had a very large collection of all kinds, but the superhero genre was my favorite. I also read the entire Wizard of Oz series. As a teenager I read all of the James Bond books.

Why did you write your historical books?

In doing my genealogical research I could not find books covering the early histories of Europe or Canada.

What motivated you to write a book targeting young adults?

My high school math and science students asked questions about content not covered in their classes.

Which of your books would you want to be the most successful?

My books showing how science supports the story of the Bible.

What books do you have in your library that very few other people would have?

"Against Empathy," by Paul Bloom. "Crusaders," by Dan Jones. "The Calculus Gallery," by William Dunham.

Why did you write your genealogical books?

Genealogy has been a life long personal hobby. I am fascinated by the biographies of the common people who shaped our history. I visited many cemeteries in multiple states over the years.

Sarina Siebenaler
Inspiring Imaginations Through Words and Art

PHOTO: *"Creating whimsical worlds, one giggle at a time."*
- Sarina Siebenaler

A Writer's Passion for Children's Books and Poetry

Born and raised under the sun-drenched skies of Arizona, Sarina Siebenaler found her calling in the art of storytelling, weaving together a tapestry of words and illustrations that captivate young minds. Her life is a blend of family, creativity, and a deep-seated love for nurturing childhood literacy.

Within the walls of her Arizona home, Sarina resides with her loving husband, three vibrant children, and their cherished rescued Goldendoodle. Her household hums with creativity, laughter, and an endless source of inspiration drawn from the boundless imagination of her kids.

Driven by an unwavering passion for poetry, art, and the enchantment found in children's literature, Sarina embarked on a writing journey illuminated by the desire to craft stories that not only entertain but also educate and uplift. Her dedication to creating children's books stems from the belief that these stories serve as pillars in fostering literacy skills, sparking the fire of imagination, and nurturing social and emotional development in young readers.

Sarina's creative compass is guided by the belief that humor, skillfully woven into the pages of picture books, acts as a beacon, drawing children into the world of reading. Witnessing the profound impact of humor in fostering a love for books through the eyes of her own children has solidified this conviction. With each stroke of her pen and brush, she endeavors to infuse her tales with laughter and whimsy, turning each page into a gateway to joy and exploration for young readers.

When she isn't immersed in the world of storytelling, Sarina finds solace and rejuvenation in the great outdoors. Whether it's the rhythm of her footsteps on winding trails during a run, the breathtaking vistas discovered while hiking, or the thrill of exploring new horizons with her family, these moments outside the realm of her stories provide the balance and inspiration that fuels her creative spirit.

Sarina Siebenaler stands as a beacon of creativity, a weaver of dreams, and an advocate for the power of children's literature in shaping young hearts and minds. Her dedication to crafting stories that resonate with the innocence and wonder of childhood continues to leave an indelible mark on the world of literature, enriching the lives of young readers one tale at a time.

PHOTO: Unicorn magic in every page, sprinkling joy and laughter!
- Sarina Siebenaler's enchanting tale, Do Not Wish for a Birthday Unicorn!

What moves you most in a work of children's literature?

As a children's book writer, I've witnessed how children's literature has a remarkable way of stirring emotions and resonating with readers. Picture books often carry profound messages wrapped in simple narratives, making them accessible and relatable to readers of all ages. The innocence and authenticity found in children's books can evoke nostalgic memories for adults who read to children. Its timeless lessons touch the core of human experience. The vibrant illustrations and poetic expression spark curiosity and foster a sense of wonder, inviting readers to explore new worlds and perspectives.

Who is your favorite Children's Author and why?

That's such a tough question. Books have been a huge part of my life ever since I flipped through my first picture book as a kid. But if I had to pick one standout, I'd have to give a shoutout to my current literary crush, the author and illustrator Jon Klassen. His creations, known as the "Hat" books in our household, are brilliant. His work is smart, funny, and his artistic style, while simple, holds incredible authenticity. Very clever work!

What do you read when you're working on a book?

Children's books, of course! You can randomly find me sitting on the floor of a bookstore or library in the children's section with a cup of coffee in hand. Other writers and creators inspire me very much. My love for poetry and art between the pages of a picture book will always be close to my heart. It's the foundation of our youth that inspires

them and helps inspire life-long reading habits that become a generational cycle.

What kind of reader were you as a child?

As a young girl learning to read, I found my passion for poetic verses. Dr. Seuss's books were my companions, shaping the foundation of my reading skills with their delightful wordplay and catchy rhymes. These whimsical takes sparked my love for writing, a passion that lay dormant until I became a mother to three children.

Watching my kids eagerly anticipate our nightly picture book readings rekindles the enchantment I felt when I first discovered books. The glimmer in their eyes mirrored my childhood excitement. Like me, they were drawn to silly stories with playful rhymes, turning each reading session into a cinematic experience woven with art and poetry. Day after day, these stories forged in them a deep love for books, reminiscent of my journey into the world of literature.

Tell us about your work and what you are working on now.

I currently have two books for young readers ages (3-8). My first book is a silly and fun story titled "Do Not Wish for a Pet Ostrich!". The sequel is a book titled, "Do Not Wish for a Birthday Unicorn!". I'm working on book 3, "Do Not Wish for a Christmas Elf!". The 3rd book will be released before Christmas 2023. All three books have comedic themes that will surely bring the gift of the giggles to early readers. Stay tuned for more silly tales in the "Do Not Wish" …series!

How do you come up with the stories you write?

When brainstorming a new character,

everything hinges on how that character will come to life in the story. If I can't visualize their portrayal or establish that emotional connection, I keep brainstorming until I hit that spark. I always ask myself the following questions: How can they captivate and entertain the reader? What conflicts will they face, and how will they resolve them? And is this character relatable to a broad audience of readers?

What sets your books apart from others in the market?

Each book I write reveals a new character for the upcoming book. It's a way for me to add a surprise element and provide excitement for each new book. Crafting these surprises and diving into fresh stories is incredibly exciting for me. There are endless possibilities ahead!

Tell us what inspired you to write your first book, Do Not Wish for a Pet Ostrich!

The idea for the ostrich character struck me when my kids started dreaming of having exotic pets at home. That's when I envisioned this long-legged, skinny-necked, lightning-fast bird making its grand entrance into the story! I sincerely wish for this feathered friend and its thrilling adventure to keep bringing smiles to children's faces. I hope the tale sparks their imagination and helps nurture their emerging reading and comprehension abilities.

Have there been any hurdles during the publication of your books?

As a self-published author, I handle everything from crafting the book to its publication and marketing. Along this journey, I've stumbled upon numerous mistakes. Navigating the marketing realm, especially using social media platforms, and building my website, has been a steep learning curve. The creative process is therapeutic, but delving into marketing strategies can be challenging. It's a balancing act – time-consuming, yet incredibly rewarding too. Keeping abreast of continuous research and hard work yields countless benefits.

What are some rewards you have experienced during the publication of your books?

I have found immense joy from the love of readers, librarians, content creators, teachers, and even celebrities like Sarah Ferguson, Duchess of York, Jennifer Love Hewitt, and YouTube creators such as Storytime at Awnie's House, who've embraced and shared my books, fills me with fulfillment.

I have a genuine passion for what I do. My hope is that the books I create will make a meaningful difference in households, classrooms, and young readers. The journey may have its challenges, but the chance to contribute positively to early readers and children through literacy makes my work all worthwhile.

Unlocking Mysteries with
GRACE ALLISON BLAIR

A Journey into Einstein's Compass and Beyond

Grace Allison Blair, a Christian Mystic and award-winning author, draws from spiritual studies in her writing, notably "Einstein's Compass," a fictionalized account of young Einstein aided by a mystical compass. Her inspiration stems from chaos in her youth, guiding her love for storytelling and emphasis on transformative themes in her work. Blair's book garners interest for potential TV adaptation, and she finds resonance with characters like Jessica Fletcher from "Murder She Wrote."

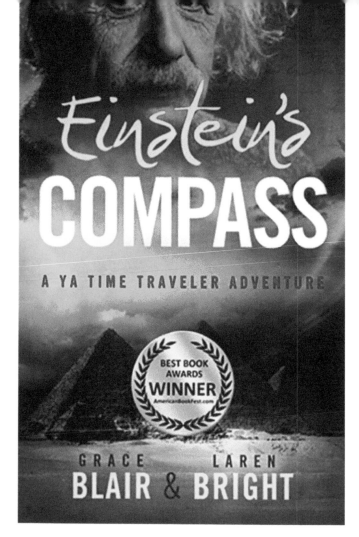

*"Journey Through Time:
Unraveling Mysteries and Embracing Destiny.
Discover the captivating story within Grace Allison Blair's compelling pages."*

Grace Allison Blair is a modern Christian Mystic and an award-winning self-help and motivational author who has assisted thousands to find their spiritual wisdom to solve everyday challenges. She describes herself as "a prime example of someone who pulled herself up by her bootstraps and took notes along the way." When she turned to writing, she chose subjects she was intimately familiar with—and their scope is surprising.

Why did you choose to write in your particular [field, genre, or sub-genre]?

Throughout my adult life, I became a serious student of the spiritual. I discovered that, frequently, psychological principles and practices lacked completeness, but adding the missing spiritual component could fill the gaps. My approach was always to see practical applications for what I uncovered in the mystical. It was through immersing myself in this field of study and experience that I came up with my idea for my book, Einstein's Compass.

Where did your love of [books, writing, reading, and/or storytelling] come from?

Growing up, my life was in constant chaos. Reading gave me an escape to people, places, and stories that kept me in a world of my own. My imagination came

alive with possibilities.

Are themes an important part of your writing, or do you allow the story to unfold them?

The human condition of relationships, conflicts and how to transform struggles into positive change.

Where did the idea come from to write Einstein's Compass, and what inspired you to write it?

Young Albert received a compass from his father when he was a boy, which gave him the inspired vision to discover his miracle theory. The compass and his quest made me create the title and a compass that was more than a direction finder rather than a vehicle of the supernatural, which Albert uses to discover his world changing theory.

I have always thought of Einstein as a fascinating person. He lived during the horse and buggy days, when the light bulb was the most advanced technology.

So how did he come up with his miracle theory, given the circumstances of his life?

What if Einstein was a star child from Atlantis?

What if Albert was trying to remember what he did as a priest-scientist during his lifetime in Atlantis.

My book of fiction follows his biographical history from age six to twenty-six and adds a new level of mystical spirituality that he had help from a supernatural compass and mystical beings who assisted him in his heroes' journey and his miracle theory. Einstein believed we must go beyond what we can see and measure in the physical world. My book, "Einstein's Compass" goes beyond what we know and adds an alternate history and possible fictional explanation for how he came up with his miracle theory and changed the world.

What is the future of your novel, "Einstein's Compass a YA Time Traveler Adventure"?

Jane Ubell-Meyer at Bedside Reading introduced me to Hollywood producer Rocky Lang, who has arranged for Rob Hedden, writer-director-producer, to write the pilot screenplay for a television series.

What literary character is most like you?

I am not sure of the literary character. There was a television show "Murder She Wrote" with Angela Lansbury. I wondered what it would be like to be Jessica Fletcher, the main character who had a life of writing books and traveling. So, I became a writer who loves to travel.

Is there any person you credit for being your inspiration for reading and/or writing?

My husband, John Blair, has been supportive and helpful. We often sit at the kitchen table and discuss the books as they develop.

What Authors have inspired you over the years and what is it that drew you to them?

Ray Bradbury is my hero of science fiction fantasy. Whenever I get stuck with my writing, I read one of his stories. James Michener and Ken Follett for their historical fiction and how to layer a story.

What's something interesting, fun, or funny that most people don't know about you?

On my 50thbirthday, I planned and performed a belly dance in a middle eastern restaurant in Dallas. Great fun.

What is your favorite quote?

My life is easy, pleasurable, safe and, most of all, FUN!

Do you have a mantra for writing and/or for life?

Dare to dream, listen to your intuition, be kind, be gentle with yourself and be courageous in your endeavors.

"Einstein's Compassis for all ages! A young Einstein takes us on the ultimate time travel, adventure, and a mystical ride. A fantastic blend of history and fiction. This is a must-read!"

--Jane Ubell-Meyer | Founder Bedside Reading

PHOTO: Grace Allison Blair:
Bridging Mysticism and Imagination Through Words

INTERVIEW

RINA BROWN

Overcoming Anxiety, Engaging Audiences: An Indie Writer's Tale

Literary Adventures and Anticipated Releases on Rina's Horizon

Rina Brown, an unconventional writer, sidesteps social media for personal connections. Overcoming anxiety, she engaged in interviews, found success mingling, and hustled to promote her indie books, favoring bookstore visits and local events.

While her peers are living on social media, Rina Brown hangs out with authors twice her age in bookstores and in a tiny diner that only serves breakfast. She knew in the third grade she wanted to be a writer when she proudly came home with a book about 3 kittens. Before her little brother became a YouTube sensation, she would tell him bedtime stories based on characters created just for him.

Eventually, she built an entire world, and decided to write it down. She had a 300 Page novel, now what? Encouraged by her parents to publish it, she decided she had nothing to lose.

Isle of the Dark came out on her 19th birthday, and she hasn't looked back. Overcoming crippling social anxiety, Rina boldly walked into local bookstores to convince owners to carry her book. Quickly experiencing the woes of rejection, she tried again, knowing she would gain nothing without effort.

As an independent author, she realized she would need a whole lot of tenacity, music, and Dr. Pepper to stay on the path to success. Joining forces with other authors around the world, she contributed to an anthology based on haunted local legends. On her 20th birthday, she released the sequel to IOTD, "Acceptance in Ice."

Stumbling across an old comic book she created in the 8th grade, Rina changed gears completely, jumping from Medieval Fantasy to Modern Fantasy. Navigating away from monsters and horses to the streets of Chicago wasn't easy, but the characters of "Sinner" insisted on being heard.

When she isn't writing, or being bossed around by her tiny white cat, you can find her binge-watching episodes of Columbo and the original Star Trek with Willaim Shatner. She avoids technology as much as possible, stacking up notebooks filled with stories, and soars in the clouds in a hot air balloon. Her books can be found across the United States, and she has toured three times in the last three years. From spooky bed and breakfasts to dingy hotel rooms, standing in the rain offering chocolates to get noticed, to signing autographs on a dusty shower curtain tossed over a folding table, Rina is willing to meet her fans anywhere.

How did you overcome your social anxiety to tell people about your books?

When I was 18, my publisher told me I would need to meet with people, sign autographs, and mingle. I had this delusional picture in my head that I would upload it to Amazon

PHOTO: Amidst ink-stained pages and tales untold, Rina Brown, the maverick author, embarks on her literary odyssey, one bookstore at a time.

PHOTOS BY MITCH MOTCHENBAUGH

and be rich, I had no idea back then how hard this business is. I wasn't exactly a people person, so my mom came up with the idea to start an interview show on YouTube from the comfort of my home. She found people from all over the world for me to talk to, so over the next year, I came up with themes each week. We called the show "The Isle Of." I spoke with scientists, collectors, writers, artists, you name it. They helped me realize that I could get out there, talk to people, and enjoy it.

What kind of reader were you as a child?

My parents always read to me when I was young, but I have a confession. I struggle to find time to read. I have so much going on in my life right now, but I need to get back to it, and have some me time.

How does your market strategy vary from other indie authors?

Social media is such an enigma to me. I have had far better luck actually speaking to people. I still cold call bookstores all over the globe, which is interesting. I would say 1 in 10 bookstores is willing to even talk to me, because I am not a big name, but someday they will want my books. I have a booth set up at my local Farmer's Market, tucked between the French cheese guy and a lady that sells rocks. There are a handful of local bookstores that set me up with signings throughout the year, which has given me the opportunity to grow as a speaker. Last Christmas, I had my first author spotlight in a coffee shop, I was terrified.

What's your favorite book no one has heard of?

"Black Ice" by Julia Blake. I love how she took a story everyone thought they knew and turned it into a fantastic steampunk adventure.

Which writers, working today, do you admire most?

That's a challenging question! There are so many fantastic people out there sharing their talent. James Fahy is at the top of my list. Not only has he written the Changeling and Phoebe Harkness series, but he is also incredibly kind. He has supported me

from the beginning. I hope to return that inspiration to another aspiring author someday. I can't get enough of Julie Embleton, I don't want to just read her stories, I want to be IN one!

Who is your favorite fictional hero or heroine?

Ellie Haskell! Dorothy Cannell created such a brilliantly flawed character in "The Thin Woman". I relate to her on so many levels and admire how she overcomes her own insecurities to live everyday life, then catches the killer!

Why did you choose to create an older character for Isle of the Dark, Ranger is in his 70's!

Everyone does a "coming of age" hero. I wanted my character to already be established, hardened by experience. Society always claims people get old and are too resistant to change. Ranger breaks that stereotype, overcomes his personal demons, and learns to love again.

Every Author has an origin story, what would you do if you knew you were going to be the next JK Rowling or Nora Roberts?

Honestly, that kind of fame would really overwhelm me. I want people to enjoy my books, not scrutinize my breakfast to see if there is some secret meaning to how I butter my toast. Maybe I would be like Enya and buy a castle with a moat.

What do you plan to read next?

Recently, I was in Bookends, a sweet shop in Pagosa Springs, Colorado, for a book event. They have this cool section of gift-wrapped books and call it "A blind date with a book." I couldn't resist! I was delighted to open Francesca's Kitchen by Peter Pezzelli, it looks terrific.

What do you see on your horizon?

The third book in the IOTD series is coming out this Christmas, titled "Truth at Sea." I am excited to be back in Ranger and Isle's world. Some big things are going to happen that will blow my fans away. This Summer, my brother is graduating, and we are hitting the road with a suitcase and a ton of books to visit unsuspecting bookstores everywhere. Nothing ventured, nothing gained, you know?

"Brown's prose is upbeat, nicely detailed, and highly readable."

— Booklife by Publisher's Weekly

Adaptation in Intelligence:
A General's Insights into Thinking and Humanity
WAYNE MICHAEL HALL
Author of The Power of Will in International Conflict

Retired Brigadier General Wayne Michael Hall, an intelligence expert, with extensive military and consulting experience, discusses his new book on adapting thinking to the information age. He recommends Feuchtwanger's "The Oppermanns" on societal downfall and discovers Remarque's "The Road Back," highlighting post-WWI soldiers' struggles.

What's your favorite book no one else has heard of.

I stumbled on a great and meaningful book, The Oppermanns by Lion Feuchtwanger, is a story about the downfall of a wealthy Jewish family in Berlin in 1933. After the Nazis seized power in January of 1933, in a short period of time they infiltrated all aspects of society some of which adversely influences the lives of all Jewish people in Germany. The speed in which the Jews were robbed, stripped of their lives, deprived of due process of the law, and shunned from all aspects of society was breathtaking to me, the reader, and to the victims. After all, the Oppermanns and many other wealthy and educated Jews thought of themselves as fully assimilated in the German society and were first of all German. Their friends and relatives had fought and shed blood for the fatherland in World War One and they had culturally enriched German life for centuries. Even with their wealth, they were overtaken by events, confused when faced with unthinkable choices, and some, like the author, Feuchtwanger, left the country, and some stayed to suffer the awful fate of German Jews from 1933-1945. After reading this book, I found that I had an increased sensitivity not to assume away any erosion of one's civil rights, comfort, and status in society. What happened in the 1930s-1940s in Germany can happen if educated people turn a blind eye to the forces that rob them of their safety and liberty similar to the despair and sense of helplessness as Orwell espoused in his book 1984.

Are there any classic novels that you only recently read for the first time?

I have read and reread All Quiet On The Western Front by Erich Maria Remarque several times, and I have seen variations of movies about the book several times. Then I discovered another of his books, The Road

Back: A Novel. As I read and thought about Remarque's books I firstly found what happened to the mostly young German soldiers many who suffered terrible deaths during actual battle as Remarque portrays in All Quiet On The Western Front. As I read The Road Back: A Novel, I found and pondered what happened to a sample of young German soldiers who survived the slaughter of World War One and returned home. Interestingly, when the Nazis came to power in 1933, they banned both All Quiet of the Western Front and The Road Back. Remarque had to flee Germany, and he lived in Switzerland throughout the Nazi era. The Road Back traces the lives of a close-knit group of ordinary German soldiers who served with one another in World War One. During this awful war, they became inured to death, casual killing, and they lost their innocence and became fatalists in the carnage. When the war ended, they didn't know what to do with their lives. They found, unfortunately, that the best proficiencies they possessed involved scrounging for food and potable water, surviving battle, and killing. When these young, battle hardened veterans returned to Germany, they found their homeland to be poor and starving, a sparse number of jobs, and a pop-

Wayne Michael "Mike" Hall, *Brigadier General, US Army (Retired), is a career U.S. Army intelligence officer with over 50 years of experience in intelligence operations. After retiring from the Army in 1999, he worked with military and private corporations providing consulting services in intelligence-related matters for more than 12 years. He also created a two-week intensive seminar for intelligence analysts and collections specialists, centering on his book Intelligence Analysis: How to Think in Complex Environments. Brigadier General Hall has written five books: Stray Voltage War in the Information Age; Intelligence Analysis How to Think in Complex Environments; Intelligence Collection How to Plan and Execute Intelligence Collection in Complex Environments; The Power of Will in International Conflict; and Whispers From the Arrow of Time. Brigadier General Hall holds a BS from the University of Nebraska, an MS from Kansas State University, an MMAS from the US Army CGSC, and an EdD from The George Washington University. Brigadier General Hall is working on his sixth book. It is a book about 'how to think' in the information age and thus stay even with or ahead of the rapid advances in artificial intelligence. The new book's title is: The Moral Imperative of Our Time—Purposeful Intellectual Growth.*

Retired Brigadier General Wayne M. Hall, an intelligence expert,

ulace that did not know what they had endured on the battlefield. Thus, they became even more despondent than when they started the physical road back to home. One committed suicide, others went to work or attended school to pick up where they left off when the government drafted them out of school into the fight. As they tried to cope, they found incongruity with their current experience level and personas and conditions at home. They sadly discovered that they didn't fit well with society anymore and could not relate to the people they left as they marched off to war. Along with the death and horrible wounding of their physical bodies and those of their lost friends, they found that they were psychologically and morally assaulted and damaged. Some of them made it, others died of their wounds, and still others died mentally and morally. Nonetheless, some of them came to rely on their inner spark, inner strength, and friendships and thus proceeded to start over and tried to adjust. Incredibly though, ominous and evil shaping forces were already showing as vestiges of authoritarianism, political unrest, fighting in Germany's streets whether socialists, communists, or national socialists in 1918-1920 and beyond.

Who are your favorite writers?

Are there any who aren't as widely known as they should be, whom you'd recommend in particular? I am an eclectic reader, and I have come to love a wide range of authors. Nonetheless, a few stand out to my why of reading, thinking, inferring implications, and intellectual delight. These authors and their books that I particularly enjoyed include: Ernest Hemingway: For Whom the Bell Tolls, A Moveable Feast, A Farewell to Arms; Tolstoy: War and Peace, Anna Karenina; John Milton: Paradise Lost; Robert Pirsig: Zen and the Art of Motorcycle Maintenance; Carl von Clausewitz: On War; Charles Dickens: A Tale of Two Cities; Great Expectations; David Copperfield; T. E. Lawrence: Seven Pillars of Wisdom; Gore Vidal: Burr, 1876: A Novel; F. Scott Fitzgerald: The Great Gadsby; Tender Is the Night; Harper Lee: To Kill A Mockingbird; Charlotte Bronte: Jane Eyre; Ron Chernow: Alexander Hamilton;

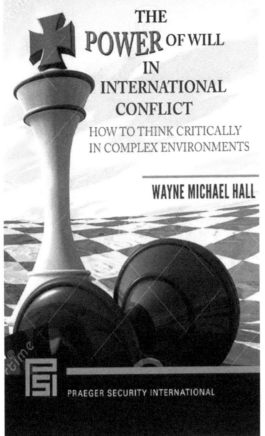

THE POWER OF WILL IN INTERNATIONAL CONFLICT

HOW TO THINK CRITICALLY IN COMPLEX ENVIRONMENTS

WAYNE MICHAEL HALL

PRAEGER SECURITY INTERNATIONAL

Wayne M. Hall's new title.

Washington; Grant; and Titan; Goethe: Faust; Joseph Conrad: Heart of Darkness; Kurt Vonnegut: Slaughter House Five; John Steinbeck: Grapes of Wrath and East of Eden; Fyodor Dostoevsky: Crime and Punishment and The Brothers Karamazov.

What genres do you especially enjoy reading?

I enjoy historical fiction such as Robert Harris and Munich; Ken Follet and Winter of the World, Fall of Giants, The Armor of Light, The Eye of the Needle; Hillary Martel's Wolf Hall and A Place of Greater Safety; Robert Harris's Imperium, Conspirata, and Pompey; and David Gilman's Master of War; and I enjoy spy novels such as Le Carrie's Tinker Tailor, Soldier, and Spy; Alan Furst's The Polish Officer and Night Soldiers. I also enjoy military history such as David Stahel's Kiev 1941; Barbara Tuchman's The Guns of August; Alistair Horne's The Price of Glory and Hubris: The Tragedy

"I enjoy historical fiction such as Robert Harris and Munich; Ken Follet and Winter of the World, Fall of Giants, The Armor of Light, The Eye of the Needle; Hillary Martel's Wolf Hall and A Place of Greater Safety; Robert Harris's Imperium, Conspirata, and Pompey; and David Gilman's Master of War; and I enjoy spy novels such as Le Carrie's Tinker Tailor, Soldier, and Spy; Alan Furst's The Polish Officer and Night Soldiers."

of War in the Twentieth Century.

What do you plan to read next?

I am planning to read The Forgotten Soldier by Guy Sajer; Emma by Jane Austen; The Pickwick Papers by Charles Dickens; The Origins of Totalitarianism by Hannah Arendt; The Russian Revolution by Richard Pipes. I must finish Benjamin Netanyahu's book, Bibi My Story, Amos Elon's The Pity of It All, and The Cognitive War by Edward Haugland.

What are some books that you were pleasantly surprised with their quality?

I came to love Jane Harper's The Lost Man. It is set in desolate parts of Australia and deals with a great mystery whose hints and threads come together slowly, as if teasing the mind of her readers, but ending in a wonderful knitting of the threads into a meaningful whole. I also came to like Armor Towels' A Gentleman From Moscow. I resisted this book because it only centered on one place and involved the life of a man who was banished to live in a lavish hotel in the center of Moscow. I came to enjoy the book because of the author's ability to make a single location interesting and because of the people, their self-interests, and human ingenuity whose minds and lives Towels let his readers peer into. I had the pleasure of reading All The Light We Cannot See by Anthony Doerr. In reading the books synopsis, I didn't see any way that this book could be interesting. But I read the book and loved it because of its intellectual and physical strands moving and spreading but appearing disjointed and impossible to knit into a whole. But the book satisfied my need to find synthesis and holism. It led me to learn about the world of the blind, the care and love for those who have gone from us, the utter bravery of humankind in the light of almost certain death, the belief in the 'diamond of the sea' as magical and not only healing one's cancer but in the German Sergeant Major's belief in finding a way to live forever. The book also took me into the horror of being shelled and bombed and caught in a huge struggle, such as World War Two, where one, as an individual is but a grain of sand.

What are some books that had a significant impact that surprised you?

One such book involved reading W. G. Sebald's On The Natural History of Destruction. It brought forth in my mind the blessing and curses being human. That is, on one hand we have this wonderful world in which we live, and humankind can and does so much good, but we are doomed to fighting, arguing and killing one another about religion, the curse of self-interest, the quest for power, and our willingness to kill each other singly and en masse. Another book that proved meaningful was Hannah Arendt's book Eichmann In Jerusalem, and her book, The Life of the Mind.

Women Business Owners are Optimistic and Confident

Consumers prioritize convenience and deals; retailers aim to deliver in 2023. PNC's survey shows optimism among women and men in small businesses, with women showcasing higher confidence and engagement in professional networks.

Above all, consumers value convenience, speed and good deals, according to new research by Sensormatic Solutions, and they can expect retailers to deliver these benefits in 2023.

Women and men who own small and mid-sized businesses are typically more aligned than they are different in their viewpoints about the economy. Now – more than ever – this is especially true as it relates to their optimism about running their businesses, according to PNC's latest Economic Outlook Survey.

Survey results show that 69% of women and 73% of men are highly optimistic about their business prospects. But women appear to have the edge when it comes to confidence – 69% say they are confident about running their businesses compared to 57% of men. This trend is consistent with last year's survey responses. In 2022, 8 in 10 women business owners reported feeling very confident in their business success and nearly half credited their confidence to their own hard work and drive.

"It stands to reason that those sentiments, together with a few key resources – professional networks, improved access to credit and the agility to navigate the economic landscape – all contribute to a level of confidence that is driving continued optimism this year," says Beth Marcello, director of PNC Women's Business Development.

Engaging in Networks

According to the survey, women-owned businesses are more likely to be engaged with the Small Business Administration, chambers of commerce and other professional groups. In fact, 83% of women business owners participate in business development organizations compared to 64% of men.

"Women often credit the benefits of a strong network to winning new business and finding new and better ways of doing business, and we're supporting that network-building through our relationships with organizations such as global nonprofit Coralus and the Women Presidents Organization," says Marcello.

Decisions for the Economic Landscape

The optimism of women business owners comes through in the survey in specific areas of their enterprises, as 64% expect to see an increase in demand, 65% anticipate an increase in sales, and 56% predict an increase in profits in the next six months. While 57% also have plans to moderately increase prices.

"These are just a few indicators of how women are thinking as they make business decisions heading into 2024," Marcello says. "While some of their optimism may be tested by continued high inflation and a potential recession, there is strong evidence that they are prepared."

Seeking Credit

When PNC began surveying women business owners in 2014, men were more likely to seek credit in the near term. The 2022 survey showed for the first time, women overtaking men when considering a new loan or line of credit to support business growth. This trend continued in 2023, with 26% of women saying they are likely to seek a near-term business loan or line of credit compared to 23% of men.

"While this data could simply reflect changes in the way women are conducting business, it's evidence that fewer women are intimidated by the traditional process of gaining access to credit for their businesses," Marcello says. "This is really encouraging."

Dedicated efforts to make more resources available to women entrepreneurs are paying off, says Marcello. At PNC, for example, women can lean on the expertise of 5,000 PNC-Certified Women's Business Advocates who have a passion for working with women financial decision makers. Through Coralus, entrepreneurs have access to a global support network and a no-interest loan program.

"Providing support to entrepreneurs and making access to credit more attainable are important steps toward their ongoing success as well as economic growth overall" says Marcello. (StatePoint)

How to Support Early Readers at Home

"Over 60% of U.S. fourth graders read below grade level due to pandemic effects. Experts suggest reversing this trend with playful learning tools and strong early language foundations."

Recent data indicate that over 60% of fourth graders in the United States are reading below grade level, with performance particularly low due to the lingering effects of the pandemic. The good news? Learning experts say that the trend is reversible. One key factor is to make sure that young children have a strong foundation in early language skills when they begin kindergarten. Here are a few tools and ideas for supporting the literacy journey at home and on-the-go:

Make Reading Playful

Interactive learning tools can go beyond drills and practice and make learning fun while building confidence and independence. The LeapStart Learning Success Bundle system, for example, features touch-and-talk pages that work on key skills like phonics, vocabulary, counting and problem solving. The attached smart stylus is designed for young kids' hands and a carrying handle makes on-the-go reading adventures possible. The system comes with an interactive storybook based on the popular animated series, Go! Go! Cory Carson, and an activity book that introduces early skills like letters, numbers and more. Sold separately is an expansive library of compatible books covering preschool through first grade subjects.

"Tapping to hear words sounded out helps children gain independent reading skills and an understanding of how print works," says Dr. Clement Chau, vice president of learning at LeapFrog. "Getting kids excited about reading through play helps set the stage for reading success before kids even learn how to spell words."

When teaching children to read, one technique that teachers like to use is to slide a finger below each word in a sentence as it is read aloud. This helps young children connect spoken words with words on a page. Slide-to-Read ABC Flash Cards are double-sided cards that fit into a screen-free tablet with special sensors so kids can explore letters, words and colorful pictures with the touch of a finger. Kids can even slide their fingers below the printed sentences to hear each word read aloud, just like how a teacher might do it in a classroom.

A strong foundation for reading starts with knowing the letters and letter sounds. One toy that introduces these essential skills is Mr. Pencil's Scribble, Write & Read. Using the included stylus, kids can trace dotted lines to write numbers, lowercase letters and uppercase letters. In addition to finding letters to build words, kids can slide Mr. Pencil across the screen to sound out new words, or free-draw anything they can imagine to inspire their creativity.

"By practicing stroke order and hearing letter sounds aloud, children will begin to map letters to the sounds they represent," says Chau.

Story Time

One other simple way to build reading fundamentals is by making your child a card-carrying member of the library. Most public library systems have dedicated children's librarians who run programming and events designed to entertain and educate kids of all ages, while developing a lifelong love of reading. In addition to programs such as seasonal reading challenges and story time, some branches also provide free homework help and host events for kids covering everything from STEM topics to music and art. Be sure to check out books with every visit!

Dr. Chau also recommends checking in with your child's teacher periodically to assess their progress in school and to learn how you can support your child at home.

"A lot of what it takes to prepare your child for future reading success can be supplemented outside the classroom, particularly with recommendations from the teacher," says Chau.

PHOTO: Marcy Bursac, winner of the G2 Overachievers Grant.

Want to Achieve Your Goals?
Write Them Down

Marcy Bursac, a technical analyst and advocate for foster care adoption, wins the G2 Overachievers Grant. Her app and platform assist in placing children in loving homes, impacting 12,000 families. Using the grant, she aims to further her mission. Remember, writing down your dreams matters.

If you have a big idea, goal or dream about helping others, writing down your vision can help. Studies show you're 42% more likely to achieve your goals if you write them down.

Take it from Marcy Bursac. After reviewing thousands of handwritten entries, Pilot Pen selected her as the newest winner of the G2 Overachievers Grant, which rewards an exceptional individual who goes beyond their everyday job and responsibilities to make a difference in the lives of others.

A technical analyst at a cybersecurity firm by day, Bursac is also an author, podcaster, wife and mother. She has used her technological expertise to develop an app for "The Forgotten Adoption Option," her book and platform that helps facilitate adoptions for children in foster care. As an adoptive parent herself, she made it her mission to make it easier for other families to adopt children from foster care, helping to place as many as possible in loving homes.

"Some types of adoption are cost-prohibitive for many families and can take years," says Bursac. "The reality is that there are thousands of children who need a forever family today, and foster care adoption is an option that can make this dream more financially affordable for more families."

Marcy has already helped more than 12,000 families through the foster care adoption process. She plans to use the grant money to fund her continued efforts to unite children in foster care with their forever families.

Inspired? Write down your own goals and aspirations and include all the little details required to bring them to life. Be sure to reach for a high-quality writing instrument like G2, the longest lasting gel ink pen. To learn more about the G2 Overachievers Grant competition or to enter or nominate someone you know, visit G2Overachievers.com.

"We know firsthand that we are so much more likely to achieve our goals when we put pen to paper," says Ariann Langsam, vice president of marketing for Pilot Pen. "That's why we pride ourselves on both providing the tools that people can use to make a difference in the lives of others, and recognizing and amplifying the work of individuals who are making those efforts."

PHOTO: (StatePoint)PeopleImages / iStock via Getty Images Plus

Make These 10 Doctor-Recommended Health Resolutions in the New Year

The New Year is the perfect time to hit the reset button on your health and wellness. Not sure where to start? Doctors say you can make the biggest impact with small, incremental tweaks to your routine.

"It is quite common after the holidays to think about all you've eaten or your reduced physical activity and get discouraged," says Jesse M. Ehrenfeld, M.D., MPH, president of the American Medical Association (AMA). "But the good news is you don't have to make major health changes in one fell swoop. You can make small, positive health choices right now that can have long-lasting effects."

Want to get started today? Here are the 10 resolutions the AMA recommends top your list this year:

1. Get moving. Exercise is essential for your physical and mental health. The American Heart Association recommends that adults get at least 150 minutes a week of moderate-intensity activity, or 75 minutes a week of vigorous-intensity activity. Just can't get to the gym? No problem: start off by going for a family walk, taking the stairs at work or parking a little farther away from the mall entrance when you're making those post-holiday gift returns.

2. Tweak your diet to include more water and less sugar-sweetened beverages. Replace processed foods -- especially those with added sodium and sugar -- with nutritious, whole foods. Stock your fridge and pantry with fruits, vegetables, whole grains, nuts and seeds, low-fat dairy products, and lean meats and poultry.

3. A number of respiratory viruses circulating this winter can be serious and even life-threatening. Get up to date on your vaccines to protect yourself and your family. These include the annual flu shot and the updated COVID-19 vaccine for everyone 6 months and older. Vaccines are also available to protect older adults from severe RSV. New tools to protect infants during RSV season include maternal vaccination and monoclonal antibody immunization. If you have questions, speak with your physician and review trusted resources, including getvaccineanswers.org.

4. Get screened. Estimates based on statistical models show that since April 2020, millions of screenings for breast, colorectal and prostate cancer may have been missed due to pandemic-related care disruptions. Check in with your physician. If you're due for preventive care, tests or screenings, make an appointment. These measures are designed to keep you healthy and help your doctor spot certain conditions before they become more serious.

5. High blood pressure, often referred to as hypertension, can increase your risk of heart attack or stroke, and it affects millions of Americans. Visit ManageYourBP.org to understand what your blood pressure numbers mean and what you can do to get your blood pressure under control.

6. One in 3 American adults has prediabetes, a condition that can lead to type 2 diabetes if left unmanaged. However, healthy eating and exercise can help delay or even prevent the onset of type 2 diabetes. Learn your risk by taking a simple 2-minute self-screening test at DoIHavePrediabetes.org. This resource also features helpful lifestyle tips that can help you reverse prediabetes.

7. If consuming alcohol, drink only in moderation. The U.S. Dietary Guidelines for Americans defines that as up to one drink per day for women and two drinks per day for men, and only by adults of legal drinking age.

8. Your health care provider can offer resources and guidance for quitting tobacco and nicotine. Declare your home and car smoke-free to eliminate secondhand smoke exposure.

9. Follow your doctor's instructions when taking prescription drugs – especially opioids. Always store and dispose of medications safely to prevent misuse. Whenever prescribed antibiotics, take them exactly as directed. Not taking the full course can lead to antibiotic resistance, a serious public health problem, and will not make you feel better if you have a virus, such as a cold or flu.

10. Good mental health is part of good overall health. Manage your stress, get sufficient sleep, exercise and seek help from a mental health professional when you need it.

If you don't have health insurance, the AMA encourages you to sign up for coverage because those with coverage live healthier and longer. Healthcare.gov has new, affordable insurance options. The enrollment deadline for 2024 coverage is Jan. 15, 2024. Find more health resources at ama-assn.org.

For a healthy 2024 and beyond, invest in your wellness with these doctor-recommended New Year's resolutions.

![The Reader's House Issue 40 cover featuring Sarah Hilary]

The Reader's House

ISSUE 40
December 2023
thereadershouse.co.uk
Global edition

Multi-Award Winning
UK Crime Novelist
SARAH HILARY
Unraveling Complex
Crime Narratives with
Remarkable Depth
INTERVIEW ☆

A Journey of Love, Family, and Fiction
SUSAN WIGGS
#1 New York Times Best Seller Author
Crafting Worlds, Inspiring Minds
JANICE HARDY
Author, Speaker, Educator

Master Minds Unveiled
Conversations with
Today's Literary Masters:

SARINA SIEBENALER
Inspiring Imaginations Through Words and Art
WAYNE MICHAEL HALL
Adaptation in Intelligence
RINA BROWN
An Indie Writer's Tale
RODNEY BOND
Journeys Through Universes
BARBARA GODIN
Unveiling Truths
GRACE ALLISON BLAIR
A Journey into Einstein's Compass and Beyond

Available both print and electronic all over the globe.
The Reader's Hosue reaches more then 40.000
retailers (including Amazon, Barnes & Noble
Waterstones, Blackwells, and local independent
bookstores in the United States.)

Visit thereadershouse.co.uk for more

The Reader's House

Save up to 50% when you
order 10 or more from the
same issue

YES! I would like a subscription to *The Reader's House*

☐ Current Issue for $ 19.99   ☐ Includes Shipping and Handling

☐ One-Year Subscription (__12__ Issues) for $199.99

☐ Two-Year Subscription (__24__ Issues) for $379.99

☐ I am a renewing a current subscription   ☐ I am a new subscriber

Name: _____ Phone: _____

Shipping Address: _____

Billing Address: _____

Email: _____

☐ Yes, I would like to receive updates, newsletters and special offers
☐ No, I would NOT like to receive updates, newsletters and special offers

Payment Type: ☐ Cash   ☐ Check   ☐ Credit Card

Card Number: _____

Card Holder: _____ Exp. Date: _____

Please mail this form to:
Magazine Name: *The Reader's House* by Newyox 200 Suite, 134-146 Curtain Road EC2A 3AR London   thereadershouse.co.uk

Milton Keynes UK
Ingram Content Group UK Ltd.
UKHW050630020124
435290UK00001B/2